TRADE CAREERS
WELDER

by Joanne Mattern

pogo

Ideas for Parents and Teachers

Pogo Books let children practice reading informational text while introducing them to nonfiction features such as headings, labels, sidebars, maps, and diagrams, as well as a table of contents, glossary, and index.

Carefully leveled text with a strong photo match offers early fluent readers the support they need to succeed.

Before Reading

- "Walk" through the book and point out the various nonfiction features. Ask the student what purpose each feature serves.
- Look at the glossary together. Read and discuss the words.

Read the Book

- Have the child read the book independently.
- Invite him or her to list questions that arise from reading.

After Reading

- Discuss the child's questions. Talk about how he or she might find answers to those questions.
- Prompt the child to think more. Ask: Would you like to be a welder? What do you like about this trade career?

Pogo Books are published by Jump!
5357 Penn Avenue South
Minneapolis, MN 55419
www.jumplibrary.com

Copyright © 2025 Jump!
International copyright reserved in all countries. No part of this book may be reproduced in any form without written permission from the publisher.

Library of Congress Cataloging-in-Publication Data

Names: Mattern, Joanne, 1963- author.
Title: Welder / by Joanne Mattern.
Description: Minneapolis, MN: Jump!, Inc., [2025]
Series: Trade careers | Includes index.
Audience: Ages 7-10
Identifiers: LCCN 2024006332 (print)
LCCN 2024006333 (ebook)
ISBN 9798892131704 (hardcover)
ISBN 9798892131711 (paperback)
ISBN 9798892131728 (ebook)
Subjects: LCSH: Welding—Vocational guidance—Juvenile literature.
Classification: LCC TS227.7 .M28 2025 (print)
LCC TS227.7 (ebook)
DDC 671.5/2023—dc23/eng/20240212
LC record available at https://lccn.loc.gov/2024006332
LC ebook record available at https://lccn.loc.gov/2024006333

Editor: Alyssa Sorenson
Designer: Anna Peterson
Content Consultant: Todd Bridigum, Welding Instructor, Minneapolis College

Photo Credits: Florin1605/iStock, cover (helmet); athurstock/Shutterstock, cover (torch); JamesBrey/iStock, cover (flame); Tawansak/Shutterstock, 1; Yuthtana artkla/Shutterstock, 3; dedek/Shutterstock, 4; Funtay/Shutterstock, 5; William Morgan/Alamy, 6-7; Olaf Doering/Alamy, 8-9; Adrian Collins, 9; Alexander Bayurov/iStock, 10; andresr/iStock, 11; Wavebreak Media/Shutterstock, 12-13; GrapeImages/Shutterstock, 14-15; Berkut34/Dreamstime, 16-17; Berkut_34/iStock, 18; hobo_018/iStock, 19; SuperStock/Alamy, 20-21; Aleksandr Veremeev/Shutterstock, 23.

Printed in the United States of America at Corporate Graphics in North Mankato, Minnesota.

TABLE OF CONTENTS

CHAPTER 1
What Is a Welder?....................................4

CHAPTER 2
Learning the Trade................................10

CHAPTER 3
Where They Work..................................18

ACTIVITIES & TOOLS
Try This!..22
Glossary..23
Index...24
To Learn More.......................................24

CHAPTER 1
WHAT IS A WELDER?

Welders **weld** metal. How? They use tools like torches. A torch uses heat to melt metal pieces.

4 CHAPTER 1

weld

The melted metals mix together. They cool and harden. They make a weld. The weld is strong. It won't break.

CHAPTER 1 — 5

frame

6　CHAPTER 1

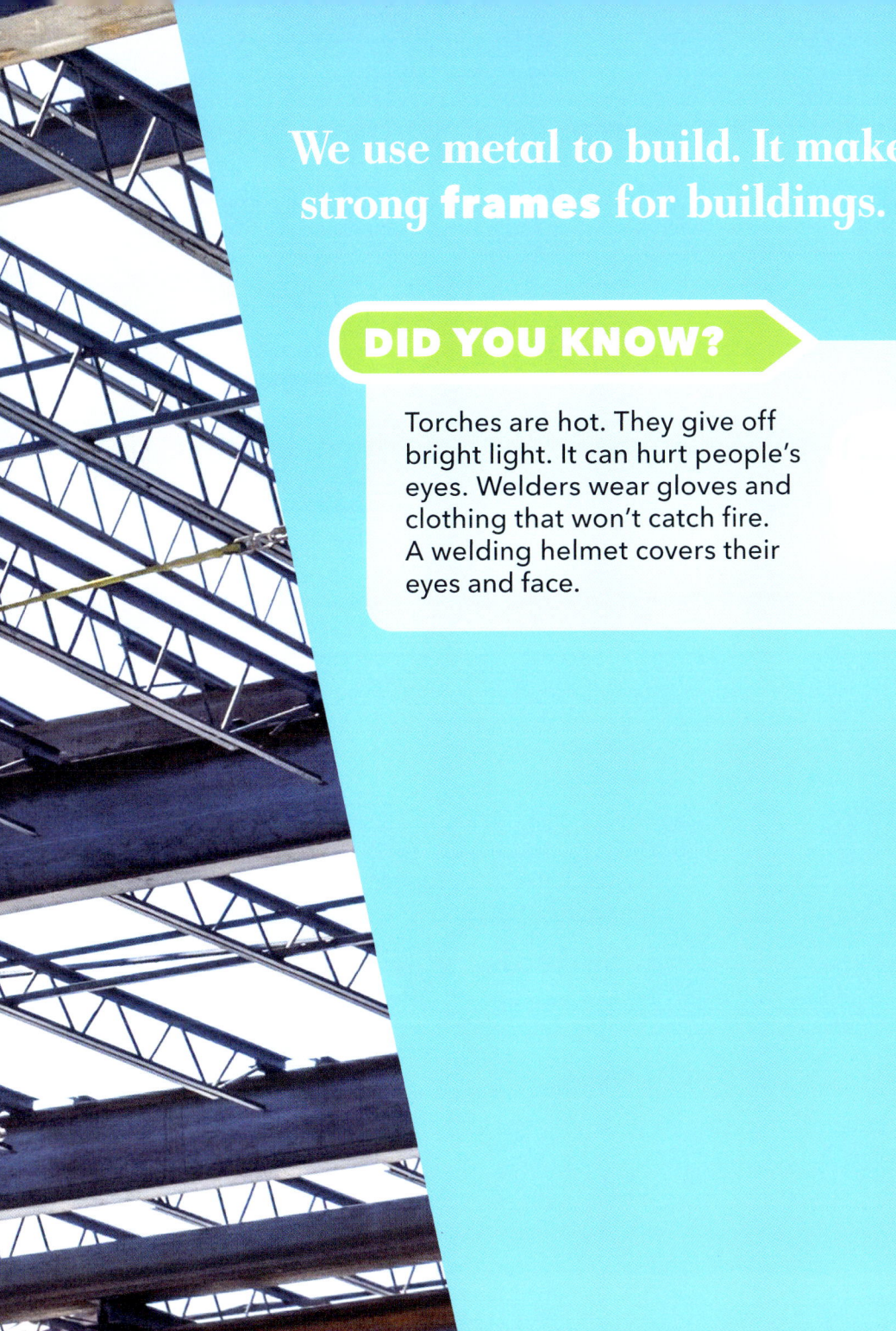

We use metal to build. It makes strong **frames** for buildings.

DID YOU KNOW?

Torches are hot. They give off bright light. It can hurt people's eyes. Welders wear gloves and clothing that won't catch fire. A welding helmet covers their eyes and face.

Welders fix metal objects, too. A car has a hole in it. A welder puts a new piece of metal over it. The torch melts the metals together. They harden. The hole is fixed!

CHAPTER 1

TAKE A LOOK!

How do welders fix a hole? Take a look!

❶

They measure the size of the hole.

❷

They cut a piece of metal to fit.

❸

They set the new metal over the hole.

❹
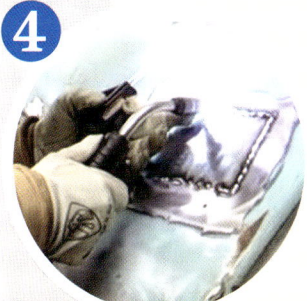
They weld small dots between the old and new metal.

❺

The metals melt together. The hole is fixed!

CHAPTER 1

CHAPTER 2
LEARNING THE TRADE

Do you want to be a welder? Welders use math. Classes like **geometry** help. Some high schools even have welding classes!

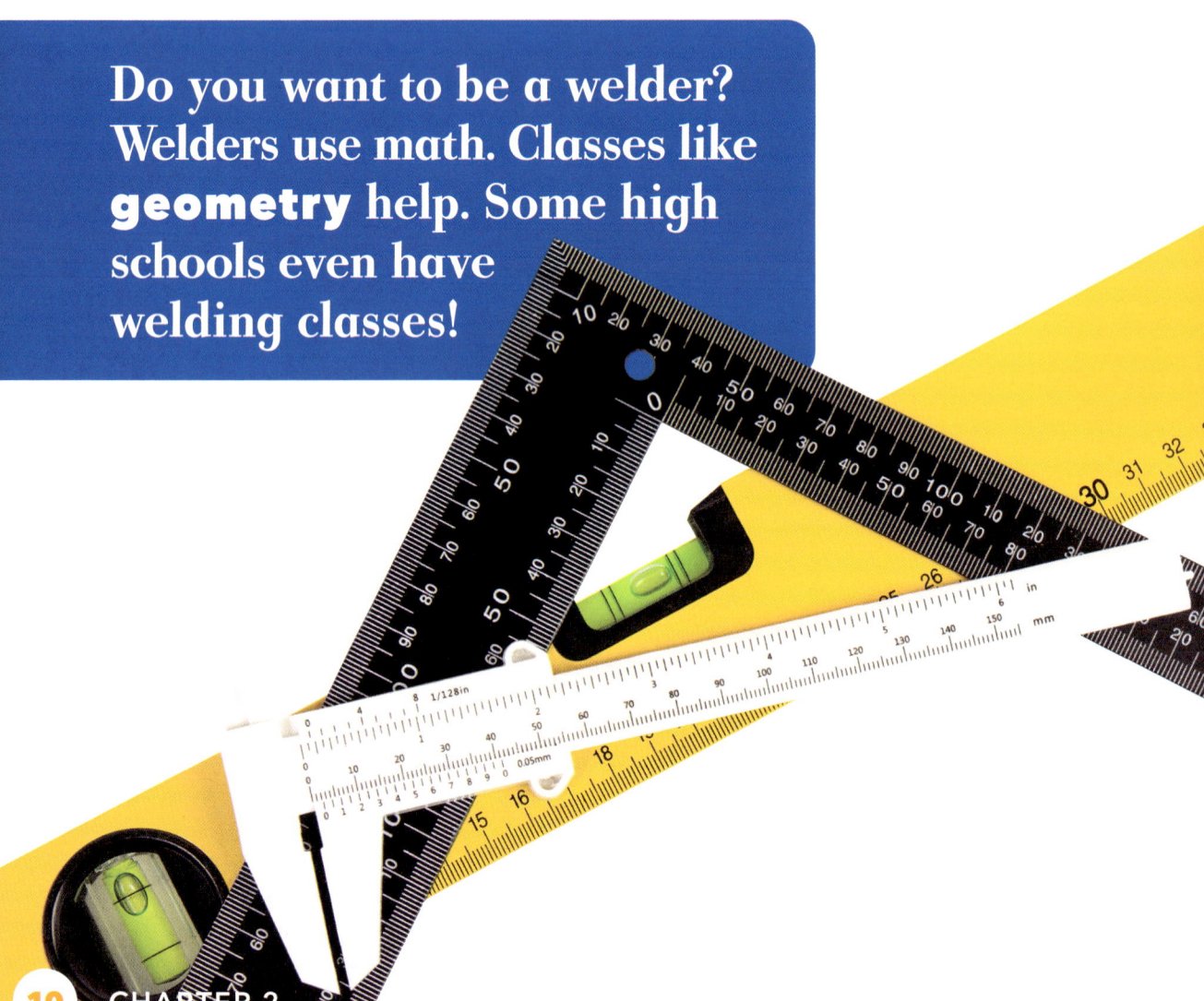

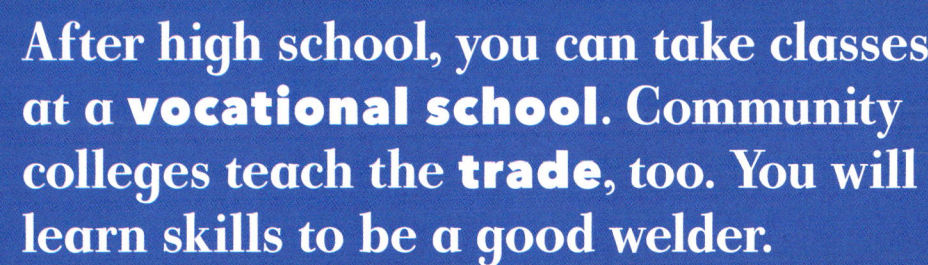
After high school, you can take classes at a **vocational school**. Community colleges teach the **trade**, too. You will learn skills to be a good welder.

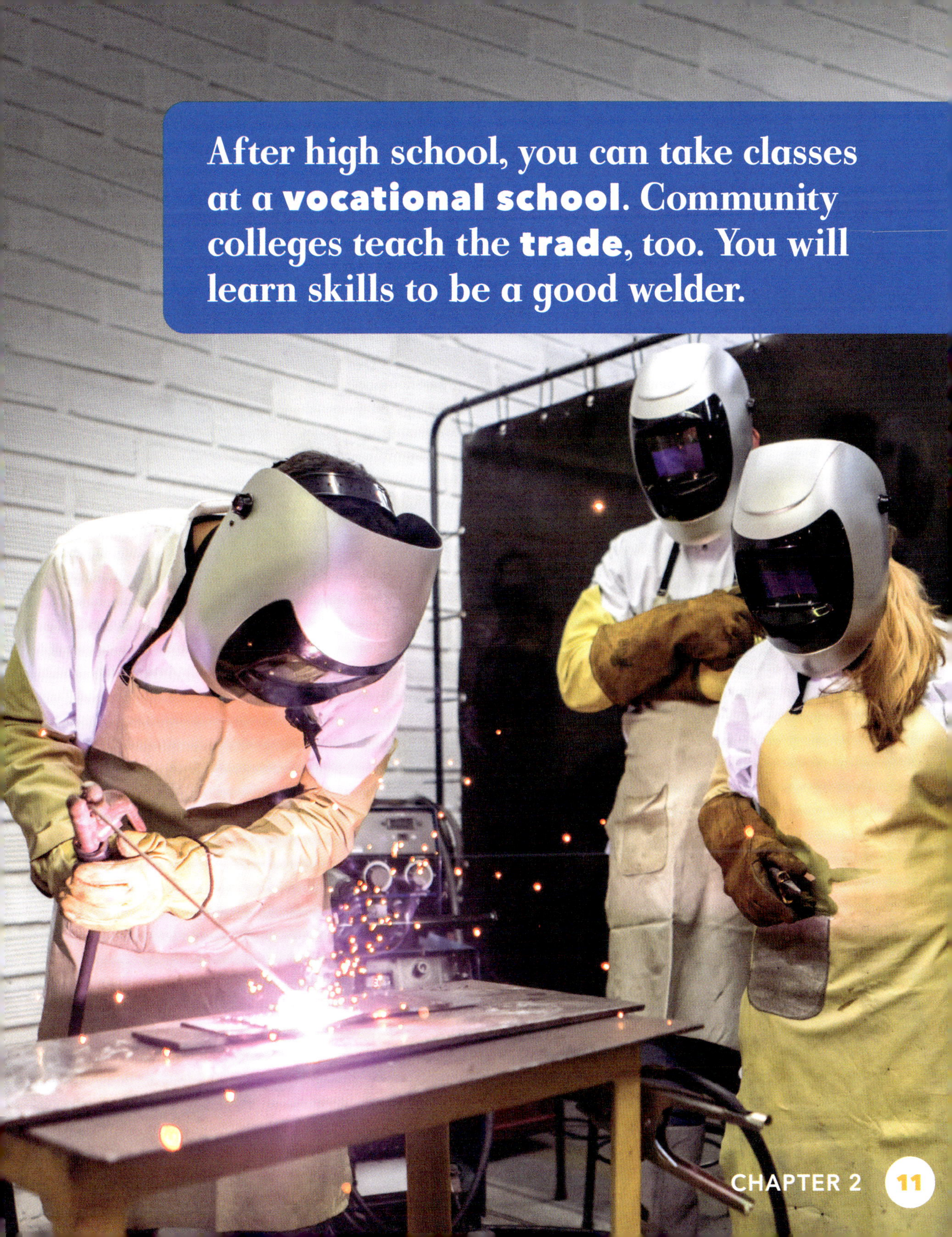

CHAPTER 2 11

apprentice

12 CHAPTER 2

You can also be an **apprentice**. Experienced welders will teach you. You will help them. You may even get your own welding tasks! After, you take a test. If you pass, you will get a **certificate**. It shows you know how to weld.

What skills do welders have? They are good at math. They measure materials so they fit just right. They read and understand **blueprints**. That way, projects are done correctly.

blueprints

CHAPTER 2 — 15

Welders are strong. They hold a torch for long periods of time. They stand and bend a lot. They may have to go in tight spaces.

DID YOU KNOW?

Welders work with their hands. They must be careful and **steady**. Why? They have to control the torch.

CHAPTER 2 17

CHAPTER 3
WHERE THEY WORK

Many welders work outside. Some work on **pipelines** or bridges. Others work on new buildings.

pipeline

Welders work inside, too. They make useful things out of metal. They create furniture. They make car parts.

CHAPTER 3   19

CHAPTER 3

Some work underwater! They wear diving gear. They weld pipelines. They fix ships or **oil rigs**.

Welders make sure metal objects like cars, ships, and buildings stay together. We have these things because welders can take the heat!

DID YOU KNOW?

Underwater welders take special welding classes. They take diving classes, too. They must pass a **physical exam**. Why? The job is dangerous. They need to be healthy enough to do it.

CHAPTER 3　21

ACTIVITIES & TOOLS

TRY THIS!

JOIN OBJECTS

Welders use heat to melt and join objects. But there are other ways to make objects stick. Like what? Find out with this activity!

What You Need:
- 2 small cardboard boxes
- 2 small plastic blocks
- fasteners such as glue, tape, rubber bands, staples, and paper clips
- pencil and paper

❶ **Try to connect the cardboard boxes. Which fasteners work best? Which do not work at all? Why do you think some work better than others?**

❷ **Try the same thing with the blocks. What works? What does not?**

❸ **Do some fasteners work on one object and not the other? Why or why not? Write down what you found out.**

GLOSSARY

apprentice: Someone who learns a skill by working with an expert.

blueprints: Detailed design plans that show how something should be built.

certificate: A document that shows a person has met requirements.

frames: Structures that support buildings.

geometry: The branch of math that deals with points, lines, angles, and shapes.

oil rigs: Large platforms that are built above the sea as a base for drilling for oil under the ocean floor.

physical exam: An examination of a person's body by a doctor or nurse to check the person's health.

pipelines: Large pipes that carry water, gas, or oil long distances.

steady: Firm or stable and not shaky.

trade: A job that requires working with the hands or with machines.

vocational school: A school that prepares students for trade careers.

weld: To join two pieces of metal by heating them until they melt together. A weld is a welded joint that connects metal pieces.

INDEX

apprentice 13
blueprints 14
bridges 18
buildings 7, 18, 21
car parts 19
certificate 13
classes 10, 11, 21
community colleges 11
fix 8, 9, 21
frames 7
gloves 7

heat 4, 7, 21
helmet 7
math 10, 14
measure 9, 14
metal 4, 5, 7, 8, 9, 19, 21
oil rigs 21
physical exam 21
pipelines 18, 21
torches 4, 7, 8, 17
underwater welders 21
vocational school 11

TO LEARN MORE

Finding more information is as easy as 1, 2, 3.

❶ Go to www.factsurfer.com
❷ Enter "welder" into the search box.
❸ Choose your book to see a list of websites.

ACTIVITIES & TOOLS